My Mother's Apron

by
Dr. Edward Keller

Dedication

I dedicate this book to the memory of my mother. I
dedicate it also to my wife, Shirley; to our seven
children and their spouses; to our 16 grandchildren
and future grandchildren.

Dr. Edward Keller

Preface

"My Mother's Apron" is a story about Dr. Keller's mother and the apron she wore on their early Dakota prairie farm. The time is the 1930s in Strasburg, North Dakota.

Keller creates a compelling image of his mother and her home made apron. Always present with everything his mother did, the apron was more than just a garment to be worn. It was an incredible tool used for a wide variety of tasks.

My Mother's Apron

by
Dr. Edward Keller

illustrations by David Christy

When I was a little
boy on my Strasburg,
North Dakota farm in
the 1920's and
1930's, my mother
always wore an
apron.

She began

the day by

donning her

cotton

apron.

It made her
come alive
and ready
for mothers'
work.

Self-made on her

sewing machine,

the apron had a

heavy neck collar

and strong belt

strands that tied in

the back.

One side

pocket

contained a

handkerchief

for my nose

and hers

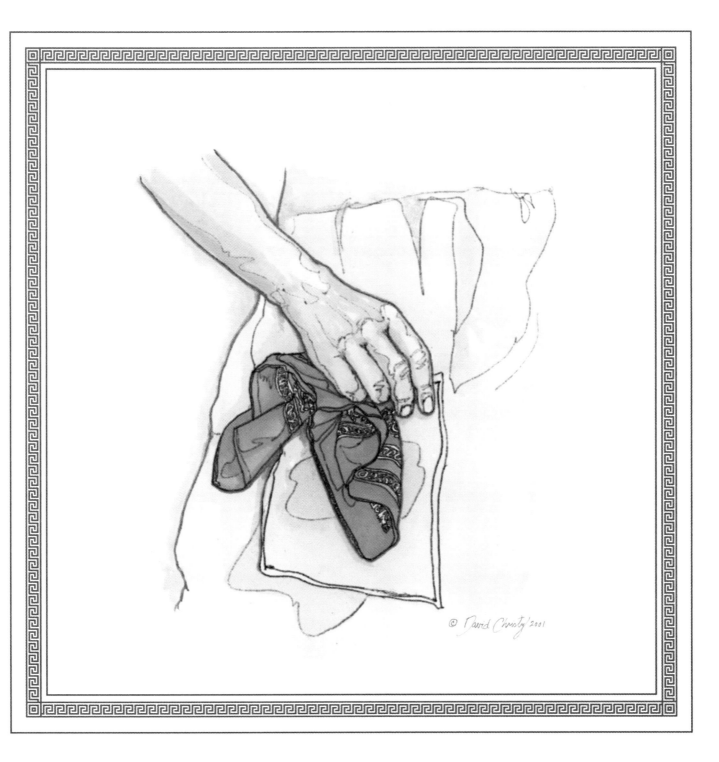

© David Christy/2001

while

the other

had raisins

or ...

© David Christy 2001

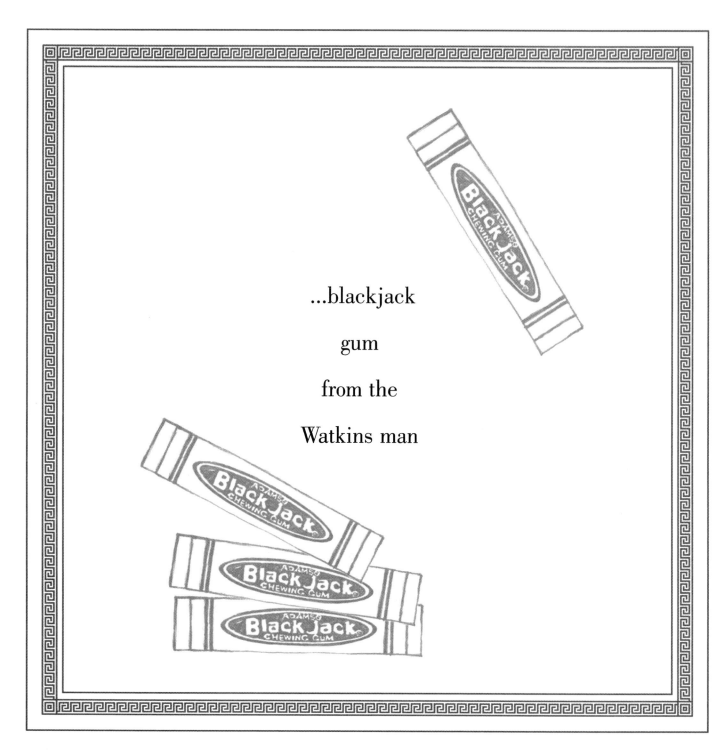

...blackjack

gum

from the

Watkins man

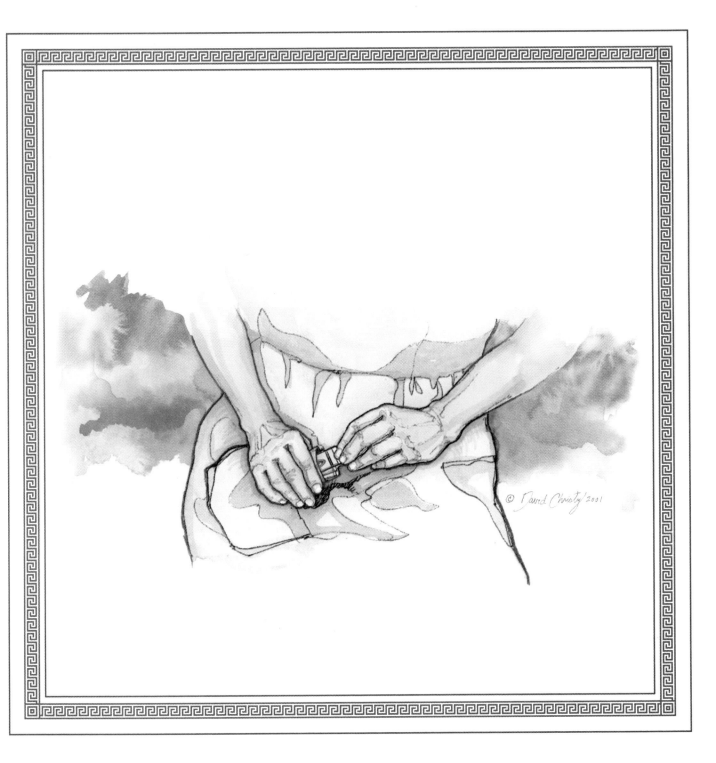

© David Christy 2001

© David Christy 2001

in case

I had

good

behavior.

When mother

brought up the hem

of this knee-length

garment there

formed an enormous

pouch which served

as a transport for

whatever needed to

be.

She carried firewood
and dried corn cobs
and dried cow chips* to
the kitchen stove.

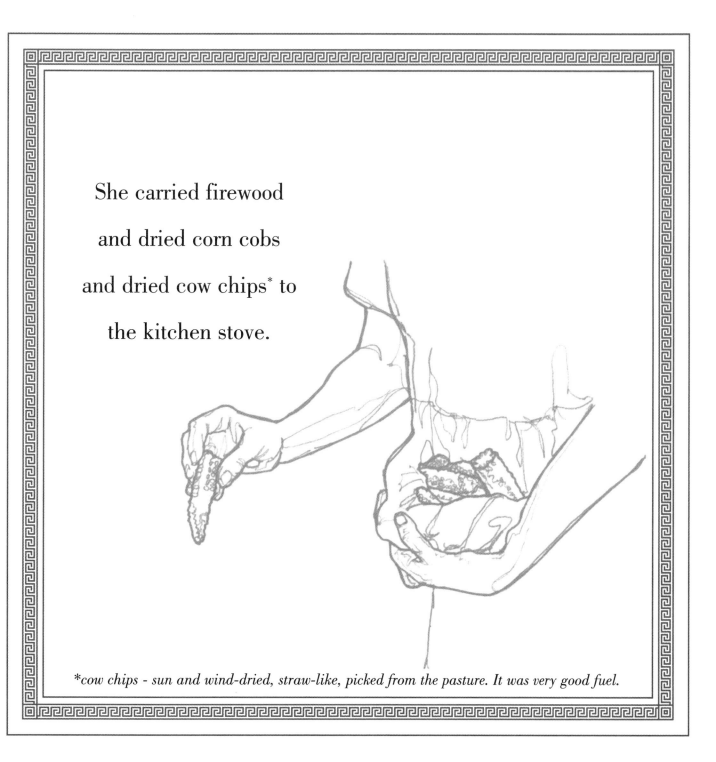

*cow chips - sun and wind-dried, straw-like, picked from the pasture. It was very good fuel.

And on another day, loaves of

bread from the oven to the pantry

in her apron.

On wash day

the apron held

clothes pins,

washed clothes

and diapers.

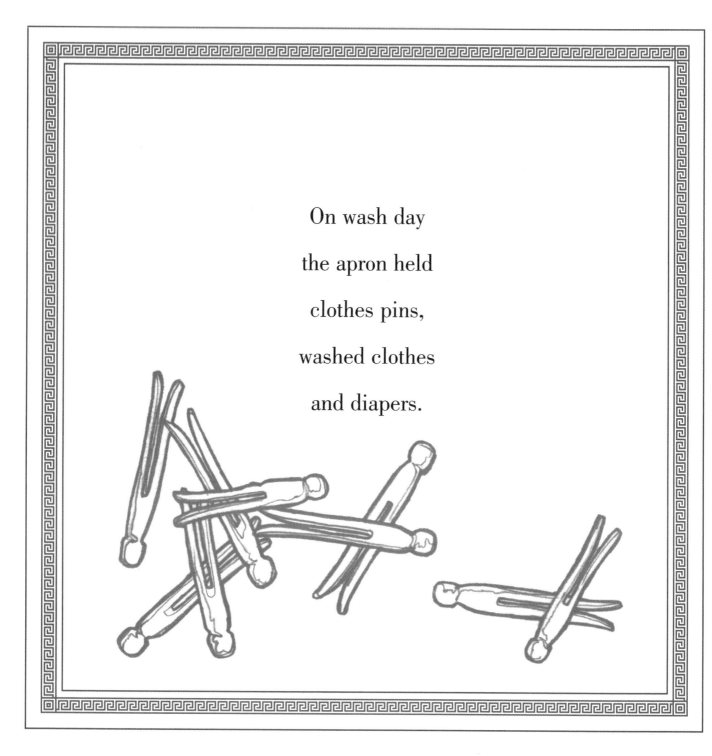

Eggs from the

hen house

cradled in her

apron pouch.

Baby chicks, baby
kittens and baby
piglets nestled
there on their way
to the warmth of
our house.

© David Christy 2001

Once a baby

jack rabbit

from the field

enjoyed an

apron ride to

become my

pet.

From the potato patch
her apron bore new
fresh potatoes. The
garden yielded green
onions, fresh carrots,
radishes and pickling
cucumbers to mother's
apron.

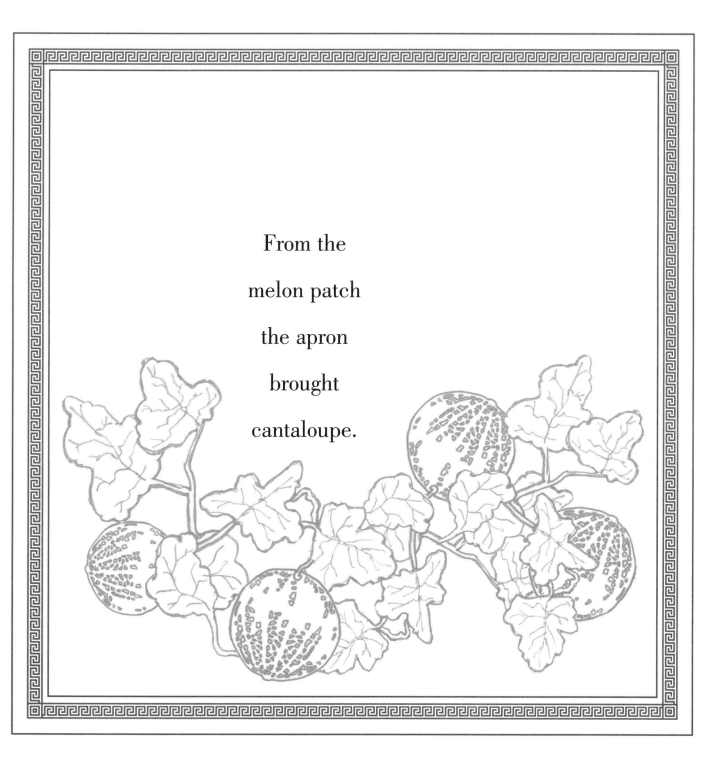

From the

melon patch

the apron

brought

cantaloupe.

The dough pan rested

in the apron on her

lap as she fingered

the dough into rivels[*]

for chicken rivel

soup.

rivels - raisin-sized bits of dough for soup noodles.

The apple pan sat

there when she peeled

apples for apple pie as

I hung on her knees

and ate the peelings.

Pumpkins being grated

with a spoon for placinda*

found support in her

aproned lap.

*placinda - a raw pumpkin mixture baked in dough pockets.

© David Christy '2001

The baby enjoyed

motherly warmth and

sweet smelling powder

in her apron

after a bath.

When my

mother

unwrapped

herself from the

work stained

apron, it was

the end of the

day.

© David Christy/2001

The only time

she didn't

wear her

apron was

when visiting,

going to town

or on church

days.

My Mother's Apron

When I was a little boy on my Strasburg, North Dakota farm in the 1920's and 1930's, my mother always wore an apron. She began the day by donning her cotton apron. It made her come alive and ready for mothers' work. Self-made on her sewing machine, the apron had a heavy neck collar and strong belt strands that tied in the back. One side pocket contained a handkerchief for my nose and hers while the other had raisins or blackjack gum from the Watkins man in case I had good behavior. When mother brought up the hem of this knee length garment there formed an enormous pouch which served as a transport for whatever needed to be.

She carried firewood and dried corn cobs and dried cow chips to the kitchen stove. And on another day, loaves of bread from the oven to the pantry in her apron. On wash day the apron held clothes pins and washed diapers. Eggs from the hen house cradled in her apron pouch. Baby chicks, baby kittens and baby piglets nestled there on their way to the warmth of our house. Once a baby jack rabbit from the field enjoyed an apron ride to become my pet.

From the potato patch her apron bore new fresh potatoes. The garden yielded green onions, fresh carrots, radishes and pickling cucumbers to mother's apron. From the melon patch the apron brought cantaloupe. The dough pan rested in the apron on her lap as she fingered the dough into rivels for chicken rivel soup. The apple pan sat there when she peeled apples for apple pie as I hung on her knees and ate the peelings. Pumpkins being grated with a spoon for placinda found support in her aproned lap. The baby enjoyed motherly warmth and sweet smelling powder in her apron after a bath.

When my mother unwrapped herself from the work-stained apron it was the end of the day. The only time she didn't wear her apron was when visiting, going to town or on church days.

"My First World"... In "My First World" Keller tells of growing up near Strasburg and Linton, North Dakota in the 1930's. At the time Lawrence Welk was a rising star accordionist from Strasburg. Keller chronicles his German Russian ancestors from Germany to Russia to Strasburg, how they worked the land, attended schools, church, parties, dances during the Great Depression, drought and grasshoppers on the early prairies.

Self published 1995, large print, 76 - 8½x11 pages, plus 9 pages of maps and pictures, perfectbound paperback, $17.50. ISBN 0-9660833-0-X

"Memory Stories"... In 95 short vignettes, like "My Mother's Apron", "Horse Power", "Welk is Here", "The Watkins Man", "Prairie Humor", Keller evokes the wholesome, sacrificing spirit of his ancestors in the 1930's on the Dakota prairies, the honorable use of what nature provided and the far-reaching effects of faith.

Self published 1997, large print, 158 - 8½x11 pages, perfectbound paperback, $17.50. ISBN 0-9660833-1-8

Audio Cassette Book of "Memory Stories"...
90 minute, 33 story cassette tape, read by Earl Ackerman, radio personality, KRRB FM, Dickinson, North Dakota.

Self published 1998, $16.00.
ISBN 0-9660833-2-6

Early
Dakota
Prairie
Series